108 Quotes
on Bliss

Amma

108 Quotes on Bliss

Published by:

    Amrita Books

    Amrita Enterprises Private Limited

    Amritapuri P.O.

    Kollam, Kerala 690 525

    India

    Email: inform@amritapuri.org

    Website: www.amritapuri.org

First edition: April 2015

1

Children, we are the light of the Divine — the eternally free, infinite and blissful Atman (True Self). Proceed with innocence, effort and faith and you will discover the bliss of the Self within you.

2

The Divine is present in everyone, in all beings, in everything. Like space, God is everywhere, all pervading, all powerful and all knowing. God is the principle of life, the inner light of consciousness, and pure bliss awareness. It is your very own Self. You can understand the secret of bliss when you contemplate the nature of the Self. When the waves of the mind subside you will see that everything you seek is already within you.

3

Whenever you feel inspired and have the time, sit in solitude and try to visualise everything as pure light and bliss consciousness.

4

It is good for spiritual seekers to spend some time looking skywards. Beholding the vastness of the sky, try to merge in that formless expansiveness, where there is only undivided bliss.

5

Look within, observe the thoughts, and trace them back to their source. Always be convinced, 'I am the nature of Sat-chit-ananda (pure being-awareness-bliss).'

6

This human birth is intended for the purpose of realising our true nature: infinite happiness. Do not miss out on the precious opportunity to find your eternally blissful Self by running behind temporary joys.

7

A musk deer searches for the source of the fragrance of musk, but however long it searches, it will never find it because the fragrance comes from within itself. Similarly, bliss is not to be found on the outside; it exists within. Once we contemplate this, and develop enough detachment, the mind will stop running after external pleasures.

8

If we can give up the attitude of 'I' and 'mine,' then there is no more sorrow and we can enjoy the infinite bliss abiding within. But we have to give up the attitude of 'I' as an individual. Happiness is within everyone, but we are not able to experience it because of our ego's likes and dislikes.

9

Children, bliss is our true nature, not sorrow. But something has happened to us where everything has been turned upside down. Happiness has become a 'strange' mood while sorrow is considered to be natural. Real bliss will be attained only when we can discriminate between the eternal and the non-eternal.

10

All of us are searching for eternal bliss, but we will not get it from perishable objects. How can anyone who is looking for happiness in the things of the world attain the bliss that doesn't belong to this world?

11

The happiness that we gain from the outer world is fleeting; it never stays with us for long. It is there one moment and gone the next. But spiritual bliss is not like this. Once the final breakthrough happens, where you transcend the limitations of body, mind and intellect, the bliss is forever and it is infinite. Once you reach that ultimate state, there is no return.

12

A man was crawling around on his hands and knees. 'What are you searching for?' his neighbour asked.

'My key,' said the man, in desperation.

Both men got on their knees to search. After a while the neighbour said, 'Where did you lose it?'

'At home,' the man replied.

'Good Lord!' said the neighbor. 'Then why are you searching here?'

'Because it is brighter here.'

Likewise, happiness is within you, but you search for it outside.

13

If you try to pursue happiness, you will miss it because the search for happiness will cause discontent. Searching is bound to create turbulence within. A turbulent mind is an unhappy mind. Your search for happiness is always in the future, it is never in the present. The future is outside; the present is within. Bliss awaits you within.

14

In your anxiety to gain happiness you create hell in your mind. After all, what is the mind? It is the accumulation of all your unhappiness, negativity and discontentment. The mind is the ego, and the ego cannot be happy. How can you seek happiness with such a mind? More seeking will only bring more unhappiness. Happiness appears only when the mind and all its egocentric thoughts disappear.

15

Happiness comes from within. A dog will bite a bone and think that the energy it gets from the blood of its own wounded gums is from the bone. We are also similarly deluded when we think that the bliss we get from within is coming from an external object.

16

All along we have been thinking that the body and the mind are real. This has caused us sorrow. Now let us think in the opposite way. The Atman is real and eternal and it is that which we seek to realise. If that thought becomes firmly fixed in our consciousness, our sorrows will vanish and we will experience only bliss.

17

To attain real peace and true happiness one has to go beyond the mind and its desires. No matter how much you may try, it is not possible to taste the bliss of the Self while at the same time seeking worldly happiness. If you eat payasam (sweet rice pudding) from a vessel used for storing tamarind, how can you get the real taste of the payasam?

18

True happiness comes from the dissolution of the mind, not from external objects. Through meditation, we can achieve everything, including bliss, health, strength, peace, intelligence and vitality.

19

Without the mind, there is no world. As long as you have a mind, there are names and forms. Once the mind is gone, there is nothing. In that state, you know neither sleep nor wakefulness. You aren't aware of any objective existence. There is only perfect stillness, bliss and peace.

20

If you vigorously keep rubbing the dust in your eyes instead of removing it, your pain and irritation will only increase. Remove the dust and you will be all right. Similarly, the mind is like dust in the eye; it is a foreign element. Learn to get rid of the mind. Only then will you achieve perfection, bliss and happiness.

21

Our problem is that we identify with all the moods of the mind. When we are angry we become anger. It is the same with fear, excitement, anxiety, sorrow and happiness. We become one with that emotion, whether it is positive or negative. We identify with the mask, but in reality, none of these moods are really you. Your true nature is bliss.

22

It is up to us to choose between temporary happiness, which will culminate in never-ending suffering and unhappiness; or temporary pain which will culminate in everlasting peace.

23

Children, sorrow occurs when there is desire. Even before creation God had said, "You will always be blissful if you go this way. Sorrow will be the result if you choose the other path." Children, having disobeyed these words, you went and fell into the ditch, and now you say that you were pushed into it. God told us about both ways. It is up to us to decide.

24

The difference between spiritual bliss and material happiness is like the difference between the water in the river and the water in the ditch. You can no doubt quench your thirst by drinking ditch water, but afterwards you will fall ill. If you drink river water, your thirst will be quenched and you will not become sick.

25

If desire were the means to attaining real happiness, we would have attained the bliss of liberation long ago. Worldly life depends entirely on the sense organs, but all of our energy gets dissipated through sensual indulgence. All pleasures of the world, whatever they are, end up in sorrow.

26

Suppose you eat only hot peppers when you are hungry, because you like peppers. Your mouth will burn, and your stomach will too. You wanted to satisfy your hunger, but now you have to bear the pain. In the same way, if you depend on physical things for your happiness, suffering is bound to follow.

27

Bliss is not obtained from exterior objects. It is experienced when the sense organs merge in the mind through concentration. Therefore, if you want bliss, try to acquire concentration.

28

If happiness is derived from concentration, it follows that it is not dependent on any particular object. Momentary happiness is experienced when we concentrate on momentary objects. Imagine then the amount of bliss gained if concentration is attained on the Lord, the eternal repository of all glory?

29

Children, experience the bliss that comes from one-pointed focus on God. If you perform your actions with your mind surrendered to God, bliss will be yours forever. Then, even occasions that would normally be painful are transformed into moments of joy.

30

Upon realising God, you will become established forever in Supreme bliss, because God's nature is pure bliss. God is neither happiness nor unhappiness. Happiness is limited but bliss is unconditional. Happiness and unhappiness belong to the world. God is the bliss beyond all duality.

31

If you want eternal and everlasting bliss, the path to God is available, but you have to work hard. If you are only interested in achieving momentary happiness, then the path to the world is open to you. To become a mere enjoyer of the items created and owned by God, only little effort is needed — not as much as what is needed to attain the bliss of God.

32

When you partake of physical pleasures, you experience a certain amount of happiness, don't you? Without controlling this, you cannot ascend to the plane of spiritual bliss. If the desires are not controlled now, later they will control you.

33

Once you enshrine the Lord within, there is only bliss, not just within but without as well. Real bliss will come to you, not the mere reflection of happiness we derive from external objects. But to attain that bliss you have to give up the so-called 'happiness.'

34

Give up something and feel happy about it. Forget that it was ever yours. To think that you have lost something is also wrong. Don't feel that; just feel relaxed, be at ease. Realise that you are free – free from that burden. The object was a burden and now it is gone. Only if you can feel the burden of attachment will you be able to feel the relaxation or bliss that comes with detachment and renunciation.

35

A truly wealthy man is one who can always smile, even in the face of sorrow. Sorrow cannot make him cry nor does he need happiness to make him rejoice. By his very nature he is blissful. He does not need the support of favourable objects or external events in order to be happy. An externally rich man may be miserable, if he loses the priceless wealth of peace and inner contentment.

36

Eternal bliss cannot be gained from wealth; only non-eternal happiness can be gained from it. Then you might ask, 'How do we live without riches? Do we have to abandon the wealth that we have?' Mother does not say you need to abandon anything. Bliss and peace will become your wealth if you understand the proper placement for what you have.

37

The world is not the problem. The problem lies within the mind. So be watchful, and you will see things with a greater clarity. Watchfulness provides you with a penetrating eye and mind, so that you cannot be deceived. It will slowly take you closer to your true being: the bliss of the Self.

38

To be content in one's own Self, by the Self, and for the Self, is what is known as inner aloneness. All spiritual practices are done in order to experience this aloneness or one-pointedness of mind. In reality, we don't have to depend on anything external for our happiness. We should become independent – depending only on our own Self, the very source of all bliss.

39

Even to enjoy worldly pleasures properly one must have a tranquil mind. Therefore children, the mind should be air-conditioned. A person with an air-conditioned mind will experience only bliss in all times and places. That is what we have to strive for. It is not wealth or any other thing that gives bliss. The real giver of bliss is the mind.

40

Understand this great truth: the happiness that comes from the pleasures of the world is a minute reflection of the infinite bliss that comes from within your own Self.

41

Before you sow seeds you have to prepare the land, clearing it of grass and weeds. Otherwise it is difficult for the seeds to sprout. In the same way, we can enjoy the bliss of the Self only if we clear the mind of all external things and direct it towards God.

42

Mother wants people to work hard in order to attain spiritual bliss. She does not want people to idle away their time in the name of spirituality. While people come to Mother for varied reasons, She will somehow make them remember God.

43

At present, God is the last item on our list. But He should be the first. If we put God first, all other things will fall into their proper place. Once we have God in our lives, the world will follow; but if we embrace the world then God can not embrace us. To have God in us is a struggle in the beginning, but if we persist, it will lead us to everlasting bliss and happiness.

44

Real gain comes from the Self alone. Only inquiry into the Self is of eternal value, and brings peace. We should know 'That' as the true bliss. What happiness is there in worrying about the mundane details in life? You should move forward considering everything to be ordained by Him. If you do so, peace will be gained.

45

There is no use in blaming destiny for anything and everything that happens in your life. It is all the fruit of your own actions. Be at peace and do your work in the present to make your future happy and blissful. Act properly and sincerely, and then if something goes wrong, you can consider it as your karma, destiny, or God's will.

46

Give instructions to the mind such as, 'Oh mind, why do you crave these unnecessary things? You still think that this will give you happiness and satisfy you? It is not so. Know that it will only drain your energy and give you nothing but restlessness and unending tension. Oh mind, stop this wandering. Return to your blissful source and rest in peace.'

47

Just like any other decision, happiness is also a decision. We should make the firm decision: 'Whatever may come my way, I will be happy. I am courageous and I am not alone. God is with me.'

48

An infinite variety of techniques around the world try to sell us happiness. They may advertise, 'Gain your heart's desire in ten easy steps,' or any such slogan to tempt you to buy their method. But what a pity! Nobody hits upon the real path except the spiritual seeker. Nowhere in the world can one learn how to die to the ego, to attachments, anger, fear, and all that keeps you from truly attaining and living pure love, perfect peace and Supreme bliss.

49

My children's happiness is Mother's food. Amma's happiness is when you find bliss within yourselves. Amma feels unhappy when She sees you depend on external things, because if you depend on them, you will have to suffer tomorrow.

50

Mother's aim is to help you reach the highest plane of experience so that you come to know who you truly are; tapas, or austerity, is meant for this. Because spiritual bliss is, by far, the greatest joy of all, the intensity of the tapas that is required, or the price you have to pay for that bliss, is also the greatest. You have to dedicate your whole life to that end.

51

I earfully pray to God, 'Oh Lord, please let me see You! You are my life; You are the Eternal One. Mind, why do you crave all these silly and meaningless things? They cannot give you the happiness, which you thirst for. These are not the things I asked you to seek.' Change will slowly come about through prayers to God and through questioning the mind.

52

Human beings have an urge to cling to everything they possibly can, even the entire universe. They don't want to lose anything. Pure love involves a tremendous amount of self-sacrifice. At certain points it may cause great pain, but pure love always culminates in everlasting bliss.

53

In order to gain pure love and the highest form of bliss, one has to undergo purification. Purification is heating up the mind in order to remove all impurities, and this process inevitably involves pain.

54

While the momentary happiness obtained from the world ultimately pushes you into the throes of never-ending sorrow, spiritual pain uplifts you to the abode of everlasting bliss and peace.

55

Inner peace always follows in the wake of pain. To reach the state of joy, you first have to experience pain. Pain in the beginning and lasting happiness at the end is far superior to happiness in the beginning and long-lasting pain at the end. Pain is an unavoidable part of life. Without having suffered in some way, you cannot truly experience or appreciate peace and happiness.

56

Once the Master begins to operate He is not going to let you go, because no doctor will let his patient run away before the operation is over. The surgery performed by the Satguru is not very painful, compared to the worst condition of your disease, and in relation to the highest bliss and the other benefits that you will gain. Since the true Master is one with God, basking in Her overflowing love and compassion helps tremendously to lessen the pain.

57

The Master is not a pain giver; She is a painkiller. Her intention is not to give you temporary relief, but permanent relief – forever. But for some reason, many people want to keep their pain. Even though Supreme bliss is our nature, it seems that in their present mental state, people enjoy their pain, as if it has become a natural part of them.

58

Pain in the beginning is the price you have to pay for the happiness you enjoy in life. Even in a worldly sense, the intensity of the pain or sacrifice you have to undergo, varies according to the measure of happiness you seek. But the happiness of spiritual bliss is the highest and most everlasting. Therefore, it is very expensive, and in order to attain it, you need to give up the lower and less pleasure-giving things.

59

Even if all the people in the world were to love us, even then, we would not get an infinitesimal amount of the bliss that we get from God's love.

60

Just as the flower falls away when the fruit takes shape, worldly desires will disappear when detachment ripens. No desire can bind such a person afterwards, whether he lives at home or in the forest. One who has established God-realisation as his goal will not attach any importance to anything else. He has already understood that nothing physical is permanent and that real bliss is within.

61

Unwise attachments to the world, resulting from our wrong understandings, cause us to lead life unconsciously, even though we are moving and breathing. Once all these attachments are dropped, everything in life, even death itself, can turn into a blissful experience.

62

*V*airagya, or dispassion, is when we renounce worldly things, realising, 'All the joy I get from outside of myself is transitory, and will later cause me suffering. The happiness I get from worldly objects isn't permanent; it is momentary and therefore unreal.' To experience real happiness, however, it isn't enough for us to just renounce the illusory things of the world; we also have to attain what is real. The way is through love. Love is the way to eternal bliss.

63

Do you think happiness comes from detachment? No, happiness is born out of Supreme love. What you need in order to realise the Self or God, is love. Only through love will you experience complete detachment and bliss.

64

Those who desire nothing but God-realisation do not bother about the past or the future. Their wish is to be in the present moment, for that is where God is; that is where perfect peace and bliss are to be found. It is by being in this moment that you attain perfect stillness and quietude within.

65

Do your work and perform your duties with all your heart. Try to work selflessly with love. Pour yourself into whatever you do. Then you will feel and experience beauty and love in everything you do. Love and beauty are within you. Try to express them through your actions and you will definitely touch the very source of bliss.

66

By taking refuge in God we gain purity of heart, and with a pure heart we can constantly enjoy bliss. Surrendering to God brings peace. Yet we often tend to worship God in a way that suggests God is in need of something!

67

You can lead a spiritual life while remaining a householder in the world. If you keep your mind immersed in God all the time, you will still be able to enjoy the bliss of the Self. A mother bird will be thinking of the young ones in the nest, even when she is out looking for food. Similarly, if you can keep your mind on God while engaged in all your worldly actions, then you can easily attain bliss.

68

When you give your friend a bouquet of flowers, you are the one who experiences the gratification of giving. You are the first one to enjoy the beauty and fragrance of the flowers. Similarly, when we dedicate ourselves to the well being of others, our mind benefits by becoming pure. True happiness is derived from selfless acts.

69

To remember God, you have to be fully and absolutely in the present moment, forgetting the past and the future. This kind of forgetfulness helps you to slow down the mind; it enables you to experience the bliss of meditation. Genuine meditation is the end of all misery. The past is only in the mind, and all suffering is caused by the mind. As you let go of the past and the mind, you become established in the pure bliss of the Self, or God.

70

Children, meditation is learning to die in bliss. Just as we celebrate birthdays, let death and dying become a time of great celebration and bliss. Through meditation you can learn to let go of all clinging and grasping in life. Your entire life should be a preparation to die happily – for only when you are willing to face death happily can you truly live life happily.

71

You are not little ponds where water stagnates and gets dirtier with time; you are rivers that flow for the benefit of the world. You are not meant to suffer; you are meant to experience bliss! By flowing into a river, the water from the pond is cleansed; by flowing into a gutter it only gets dirtier. The gutter is the selfish attitude of 'I' and 'mine.' The river is God. Children, by taking refuge in God, we experience joy and peace of mind, which then flows out from us to benefit the world.

72

Look at the little birds living by the pond. They don't know that they have wings. They don't want to fly high and enjoy the nectar from the flowers on the trees around the pond. They just live on the dirt from the pond. Yet, if they were to soar into the air and taste the nectar, they wouldn't go back to the dirt below. Similarly, many people spend their entire life unaware of their true essence and the bliss one gets from loving God.

73

You can write volumes about spirituality. You can compose beautiful poetry about it and sing about it in melodious songs. You can speak about spirituality for hours in very beautiful and flowery language. But still spirituality will remain unknown to you unless you really experience its beauty and bliss from within.

74

Yoga is not something that should be told in words. It is an experience of the yoking of jivatman (individual self) and Paramatman (Supreme Self). Just as you cannot explain sweetness after eating honey, the bliss of unity is inexpressible.

75

When you become sugar, then there is nothing but sweetness. Likewise, when we are in a state of true witnessing, there is only bliss.

76

There is great benefit in following the path of bhakti (devotion). One will get bliss from the very beginning. Thus one will be encouraged to perform sadhana (spiritual practice). In other paths like pranayama (control of the breath), bliss will be gained only at the end. Just as one gets fruit even from the base of a jackfruit tree, bhakti is the path that gives fruit from the very beginning.

77

The sweetness and bliss bestowed by desireless devotion is something unique. Though advaita (the state of non-duality) is the ultimate Truth, Mother sometimes feels that it is all meaningless and would instead like to remain just an innocent child in front of God.

78

Children, the sweet and blissful feeling that one gets from singing the glories of the Lord is an incomparably unique and inexpressible experience. There is no question of gaining total and complete satisfaction in singing the Lord's name. That is why even those who have reached that state will come down and sing the glories of the Lord with the attitude of a devotee.

79

Children, pray and shed tears as you think of the Divine. No other sadhana will give you the bliss of Divine love as effectively as sincere prayers to God. Just call out; let the call come from your heart, like a child cries out for food or to be held and cuddled by his mother. Call out to Her with the same intensity and innocence. Cry and pray to Her and She will reveal Herself. She cannot sit silent and unmoved when somebody calls to Her like that.

80

The agony caused by the longing to see God is not sorrow; it is bliss. The state that we attain by calling and crying to God is equal to the bliss that the yogi experiences in samadhi. To cry for God is not at all a mental weakness, but rather helps us to gain the highest bliss.

81

Crying for God is far superior to crying for trivial and fleeting worldly pleasures. The happiness we get from the objects of the world lasts only for a few seconds; whereas the bliss we experience from remembering God is everlasting.

82

Atrue devotee stops feeding the ego and stops listening to the intellect. He only listens to the heart. Dying to the ego is real death – it makes you immortal. Death of the ego leads to deathlessness. When the ego dies, you live eternally in bliss.

83

Meditation is the ambrosia that makes you egoless and leads you to the state of no-mind. Once you transcend the mind, you cannot suffer. Meditation helps you to see everything as a delightful play so that all experiences, even the moment of death, can become blissful.

84

Birth and death are the two most intense events in life. During both of these major experiences, the ego recedes so far into the background, that it is powerless. Once you realise that birth and death are neither the beginning nor the end, life becomes infinitely beautiful and blissful.

85

The fear and pain you have regarding death is caused by the thought that death is going to destroy everything you have, all that you are attached to and all that you cling to. This clinging causes the pain. If only you can let go of all your attachments, then the pain of death will turn into an experience of bliss.

86

The truth is that death is unnatural to us. Death is natural only to the body, not to the Self, which is our true essence. Sorrow is also unnatural to the Self, whereas bliss is our natural state. But man seems to be far more eager to embrace both death and sorrow. He has forgotten how to smile. Only when you tap into the bliss of the Atman will you truly be able to smile.

87

Once you are able to see the Truth, nothing is unknown or strange to you; you are familiar with the entire universe, and you smile, not occasionally, but continuously. Your life becomes a big smile. You constantly smile at everything — not only during happy moments, but also during unhappy moments. You can even smile at death.

88

Love and freedom are not two; they are one. They are interdependent. Without love there can be no freedom; and without freedom there can be no love. Eternal freedom can be enjoyed only when all your negativity has been uprooted. Only in the state of pure love will the beautiful, fragrant flower of freedom and Supreme bliss unfold its petals and bloom.

89

Our time here is very limited. Like a butterfly that lives only for a week, spread happiness every moment! If we have been able to give happiness to a soul – even for a minute – it makes our life blessed.

90

Jivanmukti (Self-realisation) is the highest point of human existence, a state in which one constantly experiences bliss while still living in the body. In that state, the body is no more than a cage for the soul to dwell in, for one is always aware that the Self is different from the body. Those who know the Infinite; those who have realised the Truth, do not suffer; they experience only bliss.

91

Once Self-realisation is attained, some beings merge with eternity, and after attaining that Supreme State, very few of them come down. Who would like to come down after having entered the Ocean of Bliss? Only a few can make that sankalpa, or mental resolve, to descend; that sankalpa is compassion, love and selfless service to suffering humanity.

92

Mahatmas can bestow a blessing, which even God cannot. God is nameless and formless; He cannot be seen. Mahatmas give reality to the existence of God and bless people with a tangible experience of Him. In their presence, people can see, feel and experience God. They perform the greatest renunciation of all; leaving the Supreme Abode of Bliss to live in the midst of ordinary people, like one of them, while remaining in eternal union.

93

We have nothing to offer those who are willing to sacrifice their lives for the sake of the world. It is only because of their grace that we may receive the unique gift of God-realisation. We can only bow down to them with great humility, and be immensely grateful to them for coming down to meet us and helping us to evolve. These spiritual Masters guide us towards the plane of Supreme bliss where they themselves dwell eternally.

94

A Mahatma, or Satguru, has transcended all vasanas, (inborn negative tendencies) by controlling all desires and thought waves. This is what gives them the power to smile heartily and simply enjoy being the witness to everything. As they are a source of eternal bliss and happiness, faith in the Satguru helps to make you truly happy and contented – to make your life a festive celebration.

95

Celebration is forgetting oneself. The basis of all celebration is the faith that the Self inside of me and the Consciousness behind the universe are one and the same. When love and compassion fill our heart we find newness in every moment; we never get bored. When we are always enthusiastic, happy and surrendered to God, life becomes a blissful celebration.

96

Like a drop of water that falls into the sea and merges in its vast expansiveness, the devotee dives into the ocean of bliss as he offers himself to existence. Drowning in the ocean of love, he lives always in love. Fully consumed by Divine love, his individual existence is lost, for he has merged with the totality of love. He becomes an offering of love to his Lord. In that state of pure love, all fear, all worries, all attachments and all sorrows disappear.

97

Spirituality is the ability to face every obstacle in life with a smile. Having surrendered everything to his beloved Lord, a true devotee is always in a pleasant, blissful mood.

98

All conflicts and divisions cease to exist inside of a true devotee. There is no place for hatred or anger. Those who hate him and those who love him are equal to him. Not only love, but anger and hatred are also considered prasad (a blessing from God). For a true devotee, not only good, but also bad is experienced as prasad.

99

Bliss and contentment arise from egolessness; egolessness comes from devotion, love, and utter surrender to the Supreme Lord. Contentment comes only when you are surrendered, with an attitude of complete acceptance, as you welcome every experience in life with equanimity.

100

Mother sometimes tells Her children, "Your happiness is Mother's health. Mother has no health other than that." Therefore, children, do selfless service and spiritual practice, without wasting time – and attain real bliss. Your time is precious, so move cautiously, with awareness, towards your goal: Truth, Consciousness and Bliss.

101

All-encompassing bliss is there for those who dwell close to God. Once you attain this state, experiences such as happiness and sorrow, insult and praise, heat and cold, birth and death, pass right through you. You remain beyond it all, as the 'experiencer,' the very substratum of all experience, witnessing everything like a playful child.

102

All of creation is rejoicing. The stars are twinkling in the sky, the rivers are flowing blissfully, the branches of the trees are dancing in the wind, and the birds are bursting into song. You should ask yourself, 'Why, then, living in the midst of all this joyful celebration, do I feel so miserable?' Ask the question, 'Why,' repeatedly, and you will find the answer is that the flowers, stars, rivers, trees and birds do not have an ego; and being egoless, nothing can hurt them. When you are egoless, you can only rejoice.

103

Children, when innocence awakens in our heart, allowing us to see everything in its light, there is only bliss.

104

Regain the innocent, blissful world of a child, filled with laughter and sunshine. Each one of us should awaken the child that is lying dormant within. We can never grow otherwise, as only children can grow. It is good to spend some time with children. They will teach you to believe, to love and to play. Children will help you to smile from your heart and to hold wonderment in your eyes.

105

When your eyes can penetrate beyond the past, present and future, to see the unchanging Reality behind all changing experiences, all you can do is smile. Your eyes will also smile, not just your lips. All great Masters have uniquely smiling eyes. Krishna had smiling eyes. Look at Kali as She is dancing on Shiva's chest. Even though She looks fierce, there is a smile in Her eyes — the smile of blissful omniscience. As you behold the bliss of Reality, your eyes will radiate pure joy.

106

Amma had no feelings of strangeness when She came into this world. Everything was so utterly familiar to Her; when one knows everything about the world one can only smile. When one beholds the entire universe as the blissful play of Divine Consciousness, what else can we do but smile?

107

As a result of the realisation that you are not this body, but are actually Supreme Consciousness, you will wake up and realise that this dream of the world, and all the experiences associated with it, are only blissful play. You will laugh as you look at this exquisite play of Divine Consciousness. Just as a child, who is looking at the different colours of a rainbow, laughs and enjoys it with wonder in her eyes, so you will find yourself laughing with joy.

108

Oh Divine Spirit, do You see me here? May Your starry hands shower grace upon me, giving me the strength to keep remembering You and the sorrow to keep calling to You. You are my only refuge and comfort. Blissful, oh beautiful is your Divine world! Lift me to your world of a million twinkling stars!

Book Catalog
By Author

Sri Mata Amritanandamayi Devi

108 Quotes On Faith
108 Quotes On Love
Compassion, The Only Way To Peace:
    Paris Speech
Cultivating Strength And Vitality
Living In Harmony
May Peace And Happiness Prevail:
    Barcelona Speech
May Your Hearts Blossom:
    Chicago Speech
Practice Spiritual Values And Save The
    World: Delhi Speech
The Awakening Of Universal Motherhood:
    Geneva Speech
The Eternal Truth
The Infinite Potential Of Women:
    Jaipur Speech
Understanding And Collaboration
    Between Religions
Unity Is Peace: Interfaith Speech

Swami Amritaswarupananda Puri

Ammachi: A Biography
Awaken Children, Volumes 1-9
From Amma's Heart
Mother Of Sweet Bliss
The Color Of Rainbow

Swami Jnanamritananda Puri

Eternal Wisdom, Volumes 1-2

Swami Paramatmananda Puri

Dust Of Her Feet
On The Road To Freedom Volumes 1-2
Talks, Volumes 1-6

Swami Purnamritananda Puri

Unforgettable Memories

Swami Ramakrishnananda Puri

Eye Of Wisdom
Racing Along The Razor's Edge
Secret Of Inner Peace
The Blessed Life
The Timeless Path
Ultimate Success

Swamini Krishnamrita Prana

Love Is The Answer
Sacred Journey
The Fragrance Of Pure Love
Torrential Love

M.A. Center Publications

1,000 Names Commentary
Archana Book (Large)
Archana Book (Small)
Being With Amma
Bhagavad Gita
Bhajanamritam, Volumes 1-6
Embracing The World
For My Children
Immortal Light
Lead Us To Purity
Lead Us To The Light
Man And Nature
My First Darshan
Puja: The Process Of Ritualistic
    Worship
Sri Lalitha Trishati Stotram

Amma's Websites

AMRITAPURI—Amma's Home Page
Teachings, Activities, Ashram Life, eServices, Yatra, Blogs and News
http://www.amritapuri.org

AMMA (Mata Amritanandamayi)
About Amma, Meeting Amma, Global Charities, Groups and Activities and Teachings
http://www.amma.org

EMBRACING THE WORLD®
Basic Needs, Emergencies, Environment, Research and News
http://www.embracingtheworld.org

AMRITA UNIVERSITY
About, Admissions, Campuses, Academics, Research, Global and News
http://www.amrita.edu

THE AMMA SHOP—Embracing the World® Books & Gifts Shop
Blog, Books, Complete Body, Home & Gifts, Jewelry, Music and Worship
http://www.theammashop.org

IAM—Integrated Amrita Meditation Technique®
Meditation Taught Free of Charge to the Public, Students, Prisoners and Military
http://www.amma.org/groups/north-america/projects/iam-meditation-classes

AMRITA PUJA
Types and Benefits of Pujas, Brahmasthanam Temple, Astrology Readings, Ordering Pujas
http://www.amritapuja.org

GREENFRIENDS
Growing Plants, Building Sustainable Environments, Education and Community Building
http://www.amma.org/groups/north-america/projects/green-friends

FACEBOOK
This is the Official Facebook Page to Connect with Amma
https://www.facebook.com/MataAmritanandamayi

DONATION PAGE
Please Help Support Amma's Charities Here:
http://www.amma.org/donations

CPSIA information can be obtained at www.ICGtesting.com
Printed in the USA
BVOW11s1641270515

401956BV00005B/9/P